Why
are people
Vegetarian?

Ali Brownlie

HODDER
Wayland
an impr... ...oks

Other titles in this series:
Why do people drink alcohol?
Why do people gamble?
Why do people join gangs?
Why do people live on the streets?
Why do people smoke?
Why do people take drugs?
Why are people racist?
Why do people harm animals?
Why do people fight wars?

Series concept: Alex Woolf
Editor: Philip de Ste. Croix
Cover design: Hodder Children's Books
Inside design: Stonecastle Graphics Ltd
Consultant: Alex Connell of The Vegetarian
   Society
Picture research: Shelley Noronha – Glass Onion
   Pictures
Indexer: Amanda O' Neill

Published in Great Britain in 2002 by Hodder
Wayland, an imprint of Hodder Children's Books

British Library Cataloguing in Publication Data
Brownlie, Ali
   Why are people vegetarian?
   1. Vegetarianism
   I. Title
   613.2'62

ISBN 0 7502 3713 9

Printed and bound in Italy by
G. Canale & C.S.p.A. Turin

Hodder Children's Books
A division of Hodder Headline Limited
338 Euston Road, London NW1 3BH

Picture acknowledgements

The publisher would like to thank the following
for their kind permission to use their pictures:

B & C Alexander (contents) (bottom), 9 (top), 38;
Ali Brownlie 9 (bottom), 24, 25 (top); James Davis
Travel Photography 14; Ecoscene 19 (top) (Dave
Wootton), 23 (Quentin Blake); Eye Ubiquitous 7
(David Cumming), 13 (Bennett Dean), 17 (Julia
Waterlow), 44 (Paul Seheult); Family Life Picture
Library 32 (Angela Hampton); Hodder Wayland
Picture Library 4, 8, 16 (top), 25 (bottom) (John
Wright), 28 (Jim Holmes), 37 (Jim Holmes), 39 (Jim
Holmes), 43; Impact 11 (Material World), 12
(Francesco Rizzoli), 15 (Robin Laurance), 34 (Tony
Page); Oxford Scientific Films 26 (Norbert Rosing),
27 (Martyn Colbeck); Panos Pictures (cover)
(Giacomo Pirozzi), 6 (Paul Weinberg); Pictorial
Press 5 (Jeffrey Meyer), 45 (bottom) (Paramount);
Popperfoto (imprint page) (Ian Waldie), 10 (Mike
Fiala), 33 (Ian Waldie), 40 (Newsom), 41; RSPCA
Photolibrary 18 (Duncan McEwan), 21 (Angela
Hampton), 22 (Anthony S Thompson), 36 (Roger
Howard); Science Photo Library 29 (Deplanne,
Jerrican); The Stock Market 45 (top) (Michael
Daly); Topham Picturepoint (contents) (top), 16
(bottom), 30, 35, 42; Trip/BB Holdings BV 20;
White-Thomson Publishing 19 (bottom); Zul 31.

Cover picture: children looking forward to a meal
of fruit and vegetables

Contents

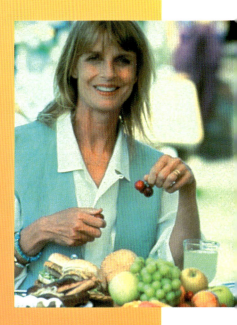

1. What is vegetarianism?

What is a vegetarian?

Vegetarians are people who do not eat meat, fish or poultry, nor anything that involves the destruction of a living animal; some people say 'anything with a face or a fin'. However, there are different kinds of vegetarians. There are those who are willing to eat eggs and dairy products, such as cheese and butter, because the animal does not have to be killed to provide these. Others, called vegans, will consume no animal products at all and eat a diet of only fruit, vegetables, beans and grains. Another group of people will only eat the fruit of plants because the act of eating the roots – such as carrots or potatoes – means that the plant itself has to be killed. These people are called 'fruitarians'.

▶ *As well as vegetables, vegetarians can eat foods such as rice and pasta, nuts and fruit, cheese and yogurts.*

t many foods
ts and even
ds as they
and lard.
and skin
es of
being
the food

f life – pop
l McCartney
d
s,

people like the inventor of
cornflakes Dr John Harvey
Kellogg, famous scientists,
teachers and shopkeepers.
Anyone may be a vegetarian.

▶ *Brad Pitt is one of many*
film stars who are vegetarian.

FACT:
The term 'vegetarian' does not come from the
word vegetable as you might think but from the
Latin *vegetus* which means 'lively' and
physically vigorous. It is supposed to describe
how people who eat a vegetarian diet feel.

The history of vegetarianism

For most of human history people have survived by being hunters of animals and gatherers of plants. Our very distant ancestors were probably mainly vegetarian because it required great skill and expertise to catch animals and fish with the primitive tools and weapons they had. It is likely that meat and fish were an occasional luxury and that people's diets were mainly composed of seeds, berries, roots and fruits that were gathered from wild plants.

Over a long period between 12,000 and 5,000 years ago, people around the world recognized the advantages of growing their own crops, such as wheat, rice and oats, and of domesticating animals, rather than having to hunt them. This was the beginning of farming. Even at this early stage animals were kept chiefly for the milk they produced and not for their meat. Killing the animal meant losing this source of food, so meat was eaten rarely – usually only as part of a ceremony or a celebration.

In India the practice of vegetarianism is an ancient and long-respected custom associated with the religions of Hinduism and Buddhism.

▲ *The San people of the Kalahari desert in Botswana are one of the very few groups of people in the world who still hunt their food.*

FACT:
The British Vegetarian Society was formed in 1847 and was the first vegetarian organization of its kind. It promoted vegetarianism in Britain at a time when the idea of choosing not to eat meat was fairly unusual, and was generally considered a very strange thing to do.

This may be where vegetarianism began as a conscious decision not to eat meat. In ancient Greece the philosophers Plato and Socrates and the mathematician Pythagoras were vegetarians, despite the fact that meat-eating was more common by this time. It is possible that they were influenced by ideas from India.

▼ *India is where vegetarianism started and where many people still are vegetarian.*

The geography of vegetarianism

As a movement in the West vegetarianism started as long ago as 1809 among members of a Christian bible group near Manchester, England, but it did not take off in Britain and the USA until the 1960s, which was the era of hippies and 'flower power'.

▼ *This vegetable market in Jaipur, India shows some of the many foods available to vegetarians.*

Although some countries are known for their characteristic meat dishes – steak and chips in France, hamburgers in the USA, sausages in Germany and roast beef in England – much of the world still lives on a broadly vegetarian diet, only eating meat at festivals or as a sign of hospitality. In Mexico and southern Africa the staple food is maize, in Peru potatoes, and in many parts of Asia it is rice. This is because these products are cheaper to buy and easier to produce and to store. Meat has to be kept in a refrigerator to keep it cool and fresh and many people in these countries do not have refrigerators.

The main exception to this pattern are people who live in parts of the world where the weather makes it either impossible or extremely difficult to grow plants of any kind.

The Inuit people of northern Canada and the Sami people of Lapland who live within the Arctic Circle, where it is too cold to grow plants, have to rely almost entirely on animals, such as seals and whales, both for their food and to provide skins to make their clothes, and bones for their weapons and tools.

◀ *Fish provide most of the diet of the Inuit people of northern Canada where little else is available to eat.*

▼ *Millet is the staple food of many people across Africa. It is pounded and made into a kind of porridge.*

FACT:
Estimated percentage
of populations who
are vegetarian

France	0.85
Germany	4.50
Italy	1.25
Netherlands	4.40
Sweden	0.74
UK	5.40
USA	1.00

Talking Points: Animal
Rights *by Barbara James*

Trends in vegetarianism

In the last twenty years or so, in the more affluent parts of the world like the USA and Europe, there has been a rapid increase in the number of people deciding to give up eating meat. In the USA it is estimated that one per cent of the population of 264 million is now vegetarian. At the same time, meat-eating has increased in countries like Japan and in developing countries where it is seen as a sign of wealth and prosperity.

However, many people in the world are not lucky enough to have a choice about what they eat and whether they want to be vegetarian or not.

▼ *Soldiers in China get their first taste of hamburgers at the opening of a new McDonald's restaurant.*

case study · case study · case study · case study · case study

Martin is 13 and lives in Copenhagen, the capital of Denmark. One day when he was four he asked his mother if what he was eating had ever had a head on it. When he heard the answer he gave up eating meat and has not eaten it since.

His family and friends are all meat-eaters. 'If my family goes to a steakhouse it isn't always easy to find something to eat. I tend to go to the salad bar,' he explains. Although some of Martin's friends think he is a little weird, he doesn't mind. He says vegetables contain a lot of vitamins so his diet is more healthy. He is sure he will always be a vegetarian.

In order simply to feed themselves, they have to eat what is available or what they are able to grow or rear for themselves. This may include fish and meat from time to time but they are not in a position to make a conscious choice about what to eat and what not to eat. The idea of having such a choice would be baffling to them and be seen as a sign of great privilege and extravagance.

▼ *A typical lunch in an Indian village of rice and spiced vegetables.*

There are several reasons why people who do have this choice decide to become vegetarian. They may wonder how meat-eaters can go on eating meat when they have been told how animals are mistreated and killed, how meat-eating can lead to health problems and how its production damages the environment. To what extent are these assertions true?

2. Religion and vegetarianism

Beliefs

At the heart of many of the world's religions is the belief that all forms of life – animal as well as human – are sacred. God, or gods, have created all life and so it is not acceptable for people to take it away at will. Even religions that do not forbid the eating of meat or fish often have sects where the members are vegetarian.

Vegetarianism is a fundamental part of Buddhism and Hinduism. Buddha, who founded Buddhism around 2,500 years ago, preached *ahimsa* – which means non-violence towards every living creature, and so Buddhists are usually vegetarian. In Hinduism people believe in reincarnation – the idea that the soul of an animal will be born again in another living form. Killing an animal interrupts its progress of evolution through the species – and you would never know who or what you were eating. So Hindus too are usually vegetarian. Jainists, the followers of another ancient Indian religion, are always vegetarian.

▲ *Cows are sacred to Hindus and are allowed to wander wherever they want – sometimes even round busy city streets.*

They believe that all life is sacred and they will sometimes sweep the floor ahead of where they are going to walk to avoid treading on any insects.

Although followers of religions like Islam and Christianity believe in the sanctity of life, their faiths do not forbid them from eating meat. Some though, like Catholic Trappist monks and Seventh Day Adventists, a group which believes in the imminent return of Jesus Christ to earth, do adopt a vegetarian diet as they believe that they should be personally compassionate towards all living creatures.

Some religions also recommend that eating a vegetarian diet helps you to be a kinder, more thoughtful and more religious person. In what is thought to be the longest poem every written, the epic Hindu *Mahabharata*, the poet says that if people abstain from meat-eating they will become intelligent, beautiful, strong and live longer in perfect health.

> 'Our parents and grandparents told us that we will be committing acts which will invite God's wrath if we harm, let alone kill animals, for any reason except in self-defence.'
> *S Jayaraman, a Hindu living in Madras, India*

▶ *This Buddhist monk in a monastery in Tibet practises a simple life of abstinence, meditation and vegetarianism.*

Religious laws

Most religions have specific laws which govern what people eat and when they may eat it. Many of these laws stretch far back into history.

In the Jewish religion there are strict laws laid down in their holy book, the *Torah*, that say what people can eat and which foods can be eaten together. It is not forbidden for people to eat meat, although there are laws about the way in which animals that are reared for food should be treated and killed. If an Orthodox Jew is unsure how the meat has been butchered and prepared, he or she may abstain from eating it altogether. Some Jewish people are vegetarian for this reason.

Muslims mingling around the bread stall at the Damascus Gate market in Jerusalem. Islamic laws dictate that Muslims should not eat any product derived from pigs.

Neither Jews nor Muslims eat pork or bacon. This may be because thousands of years ago, before people had ways of keeping meat cool, they found that pork meat did not keep well in a warm climate and that people became ill if they ate it. In Judaism there are strict laws governing how food should be prepared. Food produced in the approved way is known as *kosher*.

In the Christian religion one of the Ten Commandments is 'Thou shalt not kill'. Most understand this to mean that you should not kill people but it could apply to animals as well. On the other hand, in the Bible story of Noah's Ark, God told Noah that everything that moved was food for him, thus implying that it was acceptable to eat meat.

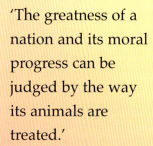 ▲ *Food, and the way it is prepared, is very important to orthodox Jewish people.*

'The greatness of a nation and its moral progress can be judged by the way its animals are treated.'
Mahatma Gandhi, Indian spiritual leader

Pure in mind and body

The belief that we are entitled to kill and eat meat is based on the idea that humans are more important than animals. Interestingly, we have different attitudes towards different animals. Some people will happily eat chicken or fish but would be horrified if they were told they were eating a dog or a horse. Vegetarians may argue that if you eat one kind of animal, why not eat all of them?

There is a popular saying that goes 'You are what you eat'. It means that if you eat fresh, uncontaminated food, you will not only do your body good but help your mind as well. On the other hand, if you eat meat from an animal that has suffered violence and been killed, then you may become more aggressive and inclined to be less kind to your fellow human beings. When we lose respect for animal life, we may lose respect for human life as well.

▲ *Rabbits are a popular children's pet, but they can also be found on the menus of some restaurants.*

▶ *These boys are taunting the bear. There is evidence to show that cruelty to animals is closely associated with violence towards people.*

There is not much scientific evidence that what you eat affects the kind of person you are. However, several religions do emphasize the need for people to take responsibility for themselves and to keep themselves fit in body and mind and they believe that one way of doing this is to refrain from eating meat.

In Eastern philosophy the word *karma* means an 'action' or 'fate'. According to *karma* if we cause pain and suffering to any other living being, we must in turn endure pain and suffering in another existence. This, the law of *karma* says, is nature's cycle of justice.

▲ *Dog meat on sale in China. The view of what animals it is acceptable to eat differs from culture to culture.*

People like Mahatma Gandhi and the famous artist Leonardo da Vinci believed that vegetarianism was a sign that people had progressed spiritually and were becoming more civilized.

"

'Finding other vegetarians to talk to was and still is virtually impossible. Through the Internet I've 'talked' with a few people, which is fun, but I know no-one at school who is vegetarian. I have to admit that being the only vegetarian amongst my family and friends is hard without someone to talk to who really understands why I am who I am.'

Janet Smithson, 16, Canada

"

3. Humanitarian vegetarians

Animals have rights

Wherever we live, animals are part of our lives, whether as pets, farm animals providing us with food, or wild animals. Humanitarian vegetarians believe that animals have rights that are equal to the rights of human beings. They believe that animals have feelings and emotions similar to those of humans, and so killing an animal is cruel and, in fact, a form of murder.

The majority of young people who become vegetarian give as their reason the fact that they believe killing animals is wrong.

▼ *Fox hunting demonstrates a particular view of animals that sees them as objects that can be hunted in the name of pleasure and sport.*

The Greek philosopher Plutarch said that if people were naturally supposed to eat meat then each person should have to kill what they wanted to eat with their own bare hands. This would be less hypocritical than expecting someone else to do it for you. Leonardo da Vinci, the Italian artist, argued that one day killing animals would be regarded in the same way as murdering people is now.

People who are very committed to these ideas may not be content just to stop eating meat. They often join campaigns to stop cruelty to animals, such as the use of animals in scientific tests on new medicines and cosmetics. Some become involved in illegal actions, such as releasing animals from their cages, or themselves taking violent action against people who conduct animal research by sending them letter bombs.

▲ *Farm pigs are raised specifically so that people may eventually eat them.*

▼ *Animals are also seen as a source of entertainment.*

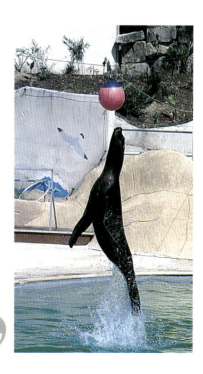

66

'We were eating roast lamb for Sunday lunch and it was the lambing season and there were all these beautiful little lambs gambolling around. Then we just looked at the lamb on our plate and looked at them outside again and thought 'We're eating one of those little things that is gaily running around outside.' And that was it…we gave up meat.'
Sir Paul McCartney in The Vegetarian Magazine, *1992*

99

Factory farming

Very few people in the world today still hunt animals for their meat. Livestock for slaughter is reared on farms or ranches, or sometimes kept in large sheds. In some cases the whole process has become so mechanized that raising animals is more like making a product in a factory.

Chickens that are factory farmed are generally kept tightly packed in sheds with no windows and only dim electric lights – often with not enough room even to turn around or stretch their wings. They spend their whole lives without seeing the light of day. Up to 100,000 chickens are kept together and fed on a high protein diet to help them grow faster. They are given antibiotics to suppress diseases so that by the time they are six or seven weeks old they are twice as heavy as they would have been if they had been left to scratch around the farmyard.

▼ *The eggs that battery chickens lay roll into a gutter at the front of the cages where they can be easily collected.*

In some countries calves being raised for beef are injected with hormones to make them grow more quickly. Piglets are taken from their mother when they are only three or four weeks old and fattened up in overcrowded pens and killed when they are six or seven months old to produce pork, bacon and ham. Animal welfare is usually far from the minds of people who keep animals in these conditions. Their main interest is making a profit.

Some people will not eat meat produced in this way. They may eat meat from animals that have been raised humanely and organically on free-range farms but this meat can be very expensive and hard to find.

▲ *Some people will only eat meat if they know the animal has been able to wander around freely and has led a good life.*

case study · case study · case study · case study · case study

A group of children at a school in England, while preparing to celebrate Diwali, the Hindu festival of light, discovered that cheese and onion crisps contained animal products and would therefore not be suitable for the Hindu children, who were vegetarians. The children wrote to the manufacturers asking them to indicate on the packets that the crisps included animal products. Strangely enough some brands of crisps such as beef and onion, roast chicken and smoky bacon are suitable for vegetarians as they contain no animal products at all.

Killing animals

It is sometimes difficult for people to remember when they are eating a hamburger or a sausage that the meat used to be a living animal that was killed so that it could be eaten. Although there are different ways of killing animals, with some being less stressful and painful than others, the fact remains that the animal is killed. For many vegetarians it is this fact alone which causes them to stop eating meat.

FACT:
Over 1.6 billion livestock and 22.5 billion poultry are slaughtered each year for human consumption. The number of fish caught and eaten every year is estimated to be in the trillions.

Animals such as cattle, pigs and sheep are killed in abattoirs. They are herded in and the larger animals are concussed with a stun gun before their throats are cut. Smaller animals are stunned using electric shocks and then killed. Then their flesh is cut up into joints to be taken to the supermarkets and butchers.

▶ *Pig carcasses waiting to be cut up and sent to shops and supermarkets.*

There are strict welfare and hygiene laws about the practices and conditions in abattoirs and many argue that the process is a humane one. The animals are killed quickly and painlessly and do not suffer. Others point out that sometimes the animals are not effectively stunned and are fully conscious when they are killed. They argue that if people who eat meat visited a slaughterhouse, they would never eat meat again.

There are many arguments about the degree to which animals suffer and whether they know what is happening to them. And is there a difference between what different kinds of animals feel? Would a shrimp, for instance, suffer in the same way that a cow may do?

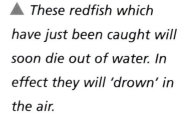 *These redfish which have just been caught will soon die out of water. In effect they will 'drown' in the air.*

"

'It's not the fact that I think it's cruel. If you think about the insides of a real animal – it's something that was living. Animals were here before us and it's not fair that we've taken over. I had a book showing sharks and whales that had been killed and that put me off eating meat even more.'

Catharine Mason, 11, Britain

"

Meat and the developing world

Vegetarianism has become more and more popular in the West in the last few years. It has even become quite fashionable. But for the majority of people in the world, vegetarianism is probably something they have not ever considered, even if they have heard of it. People in developing countries do not eat nearly the same quantities of meat as are eaten in the West. On average an American eats 120 kilograms of meat a year; in the UK the figure is 74 kg. In Nigeria this figure is nearer to 6 kg a year and in India each person eats less than 1 kg of meat a year.

However, despite this scarcity, meat and fish still have a central position in people's lives. The village of Gunjur in The Gambia lies just a short way from the coast. The women grow vegetables on the outskirts of the village and rice is grown locally in the wet season. Men from the village go out in their fishing boats every day and fresh fish is usually abundant and eaten daily.

▼ *In many developing countries, people's diets change with the seasons as different foods ripen and become available.*

'My vegetarian diet is strange to most Zambians. Africans are big meat-eaters when they can get it. And they find it totally alien for one of their kind to eat 'grass' as they contemptuously call a vegetarian diet.'

Mary Namakando, 21, Zambia

◀ *The sea is a valuable source of protein for people who live near the ocean. Fish eating is vital to their health and survival.*

On the rare occasions when the weather is too rough for the boats to put to sea, levels of malnutrition and hunger rise dramatically. This situation is typical of many other places in the developing world. People do not have the luxury of deciding what they will eat.

In many communities in developing countries the idea of hospitality is very important and meat-eating takes on a symbolic value. Strangers are given the best welcome possible and often this means that an animal, such as a goat, will be killed specially for the visitors to eat.

▲ *Chickens plucked and ready for the pot on a market stall in Mexico City.*

4. Health and diet

Were humans meant to eat meat?

People, including scientists and anthropologists, are divided in their opinions about whether human beings are designed to eat meat or not.

Evidence from fossil remains of human's early ancestors is not decisive. Fossil remains recently found in Ethiopia indicate that our ancestors from two and a half million years ago did eat meat. Bones of antelopes and other animals were found nearby that showed signs of the meat having been sliced from them with simple tools. But remains from further back in time show no such evidence and it is possible that three million years ago our earliest ancestors were vegetarian.

Most primates, such as the chimpanzees and gorillas to which humans are closely related, are vegetarian, eating meat only on rare opportunistic occasions. Many other large mammals, such as kangaroos, elephants, horses and cows, are all herbivores and thrive well.

▼ *Lions and other big cats are natural carnivores. They often eat only occasionally after they have hunted and killed an animal.*

But are fruit and vegetables really our natural food? Some scientists argue that our teeth and jaws are better designed for a vegetarian diet. Compare the smaller, flatter human teeth with the long, sharp teeth of a dog which are well-designed for pulling flesh from a bone. The human intestine is 7 metres long, again better suited for digesting plant material and grains.

But it also appears that there are certain proteins, vitamins and minerals that humans need that can more readily be provided by meat and meat products. An Australian study of Seventh Day Adventists, who are vegetarian, found that 73 per cent of them had vitamin B12 readings below the recommended level. Lack of B12 can cause serious damage to the nervous system resulting in numb fingers, memory problems and depression.

▲ *Despite their large size, elephants are herbivores, eating only plants.*

27

A healthy diet?

In the Western world it is unusual for a month to pass without the publication of a scientific or medical report about what we eat and whether or not it is good for us. For the last forty years scientists have been unable to agree on whether a vegetarian diet is more healthy than one that is based on eating meat.

In the early 1960s the American Medical Association stated that over 90 per cent of heart disease could be prevented by a vegetarian diet. Scientists in Italy and Britain have done studies which show that getting protein from vegetables rather than meat can keep cholesterol levels down. Cholesterol is a fatty substance that can cause blocked arteries and heart disease. The evidence does indicate that eating too much red meat is not good for your heart.

▶ *Buying vegetables at a morning market in Kyoto, Japan. The traditional Japanese diet, which is low in meat and animal products, is very healthy.*

In the case of cancer the arguments are less clear. It is possible that eating fruit and vegetables actually helps to stave off cancer but this does not mean that eating meat causes it. Some kinds of cancer – like colon and breast cancer – are rare among those who eat little or no meat, such as the Japanese and Indians. However, a recent research study by the Imperial Cancer Research Fund found that vegetarians were just as likely as meat-eaters to die of bowel cancer. And the high level of cases of liver cancer in West Africa has been attributed to eating locally grown peanuts – an important source of protein in places where meat and fish are often hard to come by.

▼ *The high fat content in meat and fast foods can lead to obesity and a wide range of diseases.*

FACT:
A recent study showed that vegetarians' death rate from heart disease was 28 per cent lower than meat-eaters and they had a 40 per cent reduction in cancer mortalities compared to meat-eaters. But these differences could also be explained by differences in smoking habits, obesity or the quality of the food people eat.
British Medical Journal, *September 1996*

Do we need meat to be healthy?

Some people argue that a diet that lacks meat or fish is not able to provide a person with all the proteins, minerals and vitamins that are needed for a healthy, well-balanced diet.

The human body needs protein to develop strong bones and muscles. This is particularly important for young growing children. While meat and fish are certainly important sources, protein can also be obtained from non-meat products such as cheese and eggs, which also provide calcium. For vegans who do not eat cheese or eggs, soya bean is the only single plant food that contains all the essential protein amino acids. It is a very versatile product which can be made into a liquid and used as milk, or utilized to make vegetarian sausages and hamburgers. Other beans, nuts, seeds and grains are also nutritious.

▼ *Milk is an important source of calcium for growing children. Vegans drink soya milk as a substitute for dairy milk.*

case study · case study · case study · case study · case study

Finn Davies Shaw is only two-and-a-half years old but he has been a vegetarian all his short life. This is because his parents are vegetarian and do not give him meat.

Asked if they worried that he was not getting the right foods that would help him grow, Finn's father said 'We are careful to make sure his diet is balanced with plenty of protein in yogurts and cheese.' When Finn is older his parents will let him decide what he wants to do but they would be disappointed if he wanted to eat meat.

Iron is another essential element that vegetarians must obtain in their diets. Iron helps the red corpuscles in the blood to form and without it people can feel weak and tired. It occurs in meat such as liver and also in green leafy vegetables like spinach.

Vegetarians probably do have to be more watchful about what they eat to ensure they are getting the right balance. Some take vitamin supplements – as do some meat-eaters – but if they are careful about eating a balanced diet this should not be necessary.

▲ *Doctors recommend that people eat five portions of fruit and vegetables a day.*

31

Is it dangerous to eat meat ?

Meat in itself is not poisonous. But eating flesh that is contaminated in some way can be very bad for you. Each type of meat carries its own risk to humans of disease transmission. Some people have given up eating meat for fear of getting one of these illnesses.

Since 1986 over 170,000 cows have been slaughtered in Britain because they had Bovine Spongiform Encephalopathy (BSE) or 'mad cow disease'. This disease was caused by feeding cows, which are natural herbivores, with the rehashed remains of dead sheep and chickens reconstituted as cow cakes. It is possible that some of the sheep's brains carried an infection called scrapie which in cattle developed into BSE. Some people who have eaten infected beef have developed a similar illness called new-variant Creutzfeldt–Jakob disease (CJD). Since its first appearance nearly 100 people have died of it in the UK and new cases are appearing in France. It appears to have an incubation period of 15-20 years so there may be many more cases still to come to light.

Another risk from eating meat is the possibility of getting food poisoning caused by e-coli bacteria. This is sometimes known as hamburger sickness.

▼ *A large percentage of chickens contain salmonella bacteria. These organisms are destroyed if the chicken is cooked thoroughly.*

▲ One of the first symptoms of BSE or 'mad cow disease' is when the animals lose their balance and have difficulty in standing up.

The symptoms are vomiting and diarrhoea and in severe cases it can be fatal. As many as 500 Americans die from it every year.

Salmonella is a bacterium that occurs in chickens and eggs as well as in other animals. Salmonella bacteria are destroyed with adequate cooking, but if food is not properly unfrozen or not cooked for long enough, the bacteria can cause stomach pains, vomiting and headaches. In more frail people attacks can be fatal. In 1989 it was claimed by the British Health Minister Edwina Currie that nearly all British eggs were infected with salmonella and as a consequence many chickens had to be slaughtered as a preventive measure.

5. The environment and economics

Is meat production polluting?

When we think of the countryside, of cows grazing in the fields or chickens in the farmyard, we imagine it to be natural and unpolluted. However, unless the farming is completely organic, many chemicals are used to produce meat for the market. Pesticides are sprayed on the crops which in turn are eaten by animals. These chemicals become concentrated in the animals' fatty tissues – the part of the animal that is eaten. Animals in the USA are often injected with hormones to make them grow more quickly.

FACT:
It is estimated that one cow can produce as much as 9,000 kg of manure each year. Less than half this is recycled into fertilizer.

◀ *Most farmers treat their land and animals with many fertilizers and chemicals to ensure that they will produce as much food as possible.*

By-products from the animals, such as manure and sewage which contain high levels of ammonia, seep into the ground, then run into streams and rivers and pollute the fresh water supply, killing fish and water plants. This kind of pollution can also contribute to acid rain.

Many people believe that the methane gas given off by the huge number of animals in the world makes a big contribution to the greenhouse effect and global warming by raising the temperature of the atmosphere. These may cause changes in the climate such as an increase in rainfall and flooding.

But if everyone became a vegetarian what would happen to the millions of farm animals in the world? It is an important question.

▲ *Crops are sprayed with fertilizers and pesticides which in turn will pollute the soil.*

'While our bodies are the living graves of murdered animals, how can we expect any ideal conditions on earth?'
Leo Tolstoy, Russian author

Sustainability

One of the most serious problems facing the world in the future is the wasteful misuse of the world's resources – land being a prime example. The raising of animals for meat is one of the most intensive uses of land.

Animals, particularly cattle, need open land on which to graze. In Central and South America large areas of rain forest have been cut down and cleared in order to provide grazing land for cattle which provide meat for, amongst other things, hamburgers. It is estimated that for every hamburger produced, 17 square metres of rainforest have to be cleared. This destroys the delicate balance of animals and plants, as well as driving away any people who live there.

▼ *The grain growing in this field is able to feed far more people than if the land was used to raise cattle to eat.*

In the last fifty years more than 60 per cent of the world's grasslands have been damaged by cattle overgrazing, in some cases leading to severe degradation of the soil and desertification. It can take decades for land damaged in this way to return to productive use.

Meat production also draws heavily on water resources. To produce meat takes a hundred times the amount of water needed to produce the same weight in wheat. As the world's population increases we need not only to produce more food to feed everyone but we have to make sure that we are doing that in a way that will not damage or pollute the land, making agriculture difficult for future generations. These are important issues that have to be considered for the future of the planet.

▲ *Vast areas of rainforest have been cleared in order to raise animals for the food market.*

FACT:
Sixty-four per cent of American agricultural land is used to grow livestock feed.
Vegetarian Times, 1994

Vegetarianism could feed the world

All our food comes originally from plants. We can either eat the plants directly as vegetables, fruit and rice, for example, or we can feed it to animals which we then kill and eat. Feeding plants to animals is very wasteful because only a small proportion of the plant material is turned into meat. The rest is used by the animal for the energy it needs during its lifetime to grow, move around and keep warm. Because of this, almost 90 per cent of the protein we feed to animals is lost. If this plant protein was fed directly to humans, it would feed far more people.

▼ *In the West African country of Mali millet is an important staple crop.*

Much of the grain grown in the West is used to feed animals but it is not enough. Cereals and nuts and other fodder is also imported from poorer nations. Some experts estimate that a third of Africa's peanut crop (and peanuts provide the same amount of protein as meat) ends up in the stomachs of cattle and poultry in Western Europe.

Meat feeds few at the expense of many. Far more people could be fed if land was used to produce plant crops. It takes 7 kg of grain to produce half a kilogram of meat. Put another way, for every steak produced, forty-five to fifty people could have a bowl of cereal grain.

A former UK ambassador to the United Nations, Sir Crispin Tickell, noted that if 35 per cent of our calories came from animal products – as happens in America now – then the world would only be able to sustain a population of 2.5 billion people. But if everyone was vegetarian and the food was equally distributed, the world could support at least six billion people (which was the estimated population of the world in the year 2000).

FACT:
Over his or her lifetime the average American eats:
11 cows, 4 calves, 3 lambs, 43 pigs, 1,107 chickens, 45 turkeys, and 861 fish.
New Internationalist, January 1991

▼ *These palm oil nuts are being transported from a plantation in Malaysia. They are an important source of cooking oil.*

6. Being a vegetarian

Attitudes to vegetarians

When a high-ranking US general learned that one of his soldiers was a vegetarian, he remarked 'Isn't that against regulations?' The soldier then had to undergo physical tests to prove that he was fit enough to be a soldier – which he was. This story shows that some people think that it is impossible for vegetarians to be strong and energetic. Some even consider it is unmanly and – probably as in the case quoted above – un-American!

More traditional and sometimes older people tend to associate vegetarianism with long-haired hippies wearing sandals. This is probably because it was in the 1960s – when hippies were in fashion – that vegetarianism became popular in Britain and the USA.

▶ *Martina Navratilova, who won a record 167 singles tennis titles, is a vegan.*

While this stereotype may occasionally be true, vegetarians today come from all walks of life and include business people, teachers, pop stars, sports personalities and even farmers and soldiers.

Far from being sickly and weak, vegetarians can be just as fit and strong as meat-eaters and sometimes more so. The US athlete Carl Lewis won four gold medals at the 1984 Olympic Games for sprinting and long jump. And in 1956 Murray Rose from Australia won a gold medal in the 1500 metres freestyle swimming. They are both vegetarians. So is Martina Navratilova, the tennis player who won Wimbledon and the US Open several times.

Although vegetarians are usually much better understood these days, there are still some people who cannot appreciate exactly what it means to be a vegetarian.

▲ *Carl Lewis challenges the stereotype of vegetarians as weak and feeble people.*

Vegetarianism is big business

The rapid rise in the number of vegetarians in Europe and America means that this market is now taken very seriously by manufacturers and retailers. It has become big business.

Special foods are produced for vegetarians and in Britain alone this market is now worth at least £450 million a year, a figure that has doubled in the past eight years. Once only small health-food stores sold specialist products but now all the leading supermarkets and food companies offer their own brands of ready-made convenience vegetarian meals. Food is labelled indicating whether it is suitable for vegetarians.

▼ *Linda McCartney's range of ready-made vegetarian meals became very popular with shoppers.*

◀ *Beans and pulses are an important source of protein for vegetarians.*

Most restaurants now offer a vegetarian option and several are completely vegetarian. Even hamburger chains like Burger King offer veggie-burgers (although they may be cooked in the same fat as the meat versions). Vegetarian recipe books are best-sellers and vegetarian cooking has become more popular with meat-eaters as a healthy and cheaper alternative to meat.

Cosmetic companies like The Body Shop are proud to advertise their make-up, creams and soaps as not having been tested on animals or not using any animal products in their manufacture. There are even specialist travel agents who will arrange holidays for vegetarians to resorts where they are assured of getting vegetarian food.

FACT:
In August 2000 McDonald's, the fast food giant, announced it would only buy eggs from suppliers who observed animal welfare guidelines set up by its panel of animal care experts.
The American Humane Association

A vegetarian life

The reasons why most vegetarians do not eat meat are various and often involve a combination of factors. Vegetarianism means a lot more to many people than simply eating a diet of fruit and vegetables. It is part of a wider lifestyle through which they follow their principles in other ways that affect how they behave.

The concern for their health and the environment may mean that they like to walk or cycle instead of always travelling by car; they may recycle their rubbish and eat fresh foods that have been produced organically. Of course, many meat-eaters may do this too. Their distaste at the killing of animals may mean that they are opposed to other forms of violence committed against animals, like fox hunting or the export of live animals; or they may deplore violence that involves people, like the sport of boxing.

There are other ways in which vegetarians can support their beliefs. They can join one of the many vegetarian societies that are found in nearly all countries in Europe, North America and Australia, and they can support these organizations by using credit cards which benefit them for every purchase made.

> '*Basically we should stop doing those things that are destructive to the environment, other creatures and ourselves and figure out new ways of existing.*'
> *Moby, US musician*

▼ *Will there be enough food for these children in the future?*

Being a vegetarian is one way in which people who hold strong beliefs about the way we live can show that they are prepared to make a positive contribution to their own health, the general welfare of the planet and a better society for all.

◀ *For many people vegetarianism is part of leading a healthy life.*

case study · case study · case study · ca y

Although Richard Gere's early years were spent on a farm in upstate New York, he is now a committed vegetarian. His conversion to vegetarianism came after he had visited the mountain state of Tibet in the Himalayas and met with Buddhist monks.

So impressed was he with their philosophy of non-violence and peace that he decided not only to become a vegetarian but also to convert to Buddhism. He now campaigns for Tibet to be independent from China and has started a foundation for Tibet in the USA.

GLOSSARY

Abattoir
A building where animals are killed and cut up for meat.

Acid rain
Rain containing acids which have a harmful effect on plants, animals and buildings – caused by chemicals being released into the atmosphere when fuels are burned.

Amino acids
The building blocks of proteins which are vital for growth and good health.

Ancestors
People from whom we are descended.

Anthropologist
A scientist who studies the origins and relationships of human beings.

Bacterium (pl. bacteria)
A single-celled organism which can cause disease in animals.

Biodiversity
The wide range and variety of plant and animal life on Earth.

Cereals
Grasses grown for their edible seeds (grain).

Dairy products
Products derived from the milk of animals including butter and cheese.

Desertification
The spread of deserts caused by over-grazing of livestock or climate change.

Environment
The area – the land and buildings – around us.

Factory farming
The mass production of animals and animal products for human consumption.

Free-range
System of farming where animals are free to wander around farmyards and fields, rather than being cooped up in sheds.

Fruitarian
Someone who only eats fruit and vegetables the harvesting of which does not bring about the death of the plant from which they are gathered.

Gelatine
A jelly-like substance made by boiling the skin and bones of pigs and cattle in water. It is sometimes used to thicken yogurt, ice creams and sweets.

Greenhouse effect
The warming of the earth's atmosphere that results from solar radiation being trapped in the atmosphere by an increase in gases.

Herbivores
Animals that eat only plant material.

Hormone
A substance produced by the body that causes a specific physical effect.

Humanitarian
Someone who is concerned about their fellow humans and other living creatures.

Incubation period
The time needed for an egg or an embryo to develop before it is born.

Intensive farming
Farming which uses the land to its maximum capacity.

Lard
A soft white fat obtained from animals, usually pigs.

Legume
A type of plant which has pods containing seeds like peas, beans and lentils.

Livestock
The animals kept on a farm or a ranch.

Mineral
A substance, other than plant or animal matter, which is needed by the body.

Obesity
The condition of being extremely fat and overweight.

Protein
Organic compounds which are an essential part of living cells and vital for human growth and development.

Rennet
A substance taken from the stomach of a slaughtered calf used to make cheese.

Sect
A subdivision of a larger religious group.

Staple food
The food providing the main source of nutrition to a group of people.

Vegan
A vegetarian who eats no animal produce at all, including cheese, milk and eggs.

Vegetarian
Someone who eats no meat or fish, but who may eat animal products such as cheese or yogurt.

Vitamin
A substance that is essential in small quantities to the working of the human body.

BOOKS TO READ

A Boy, a Chicken and the Lion of Judah by Roberta Kalechofsky. A story of how a Jewish boy became a vegetarian.

Save the Animals: 101 Easy Things You Can Do by Ingrid Newkirk. Ideas for action compassionate children can take.

Ishmael by Daniel Quinn. A view of human beings and their mistakes seen through the eyes of a captive gorilla.

Doctor Rat by William Kotzwinkle. Graphic detail of a laboratory rat's life (very disturbing) 13+.

The Great Kapok Tree by Lynne Cherry. Picture book about the importance of the rainforest.

Teen's Guide to Going Vegetarian by Judy Krizmanic. Information on what vegetarianism is and appropriate foods you can eat.

Leprechaun Cake and Other Tales by Vonnie Winslow Crist and Debra Wasserman. Stories about vegetarian children, with recipes.

Animal Century by Mark Gold. Deals with changing attitudes towards animals and their rights over the last century.

What the Label Doesn't Tell You by Sue Dibb. Food labelling and factory farming.

Talking Points: Animal Rights by Barbara James, Wayland.

We're Talking about Vegetarianism by Samantha Calvert, Wayland.

ORGANIZATIONS

Canada
Toronto Vegetarian Society
736 Bathurst Street
Toronto
ON M5S 2R4

UK
The Vegetarian Society
Parkdale
Dunham Road
Altrincham
Cheshire WA14 4QG
www.vegsoc.org

USA
Vegetarian Resource Center
PO Box 38-1068
Cambridge
MA 02238-1068

Veggies Unite
PO Box 5312
Fort Wayne
IN 46895-5312
www.vegweb.com

Vegetarian Youth Network
PO Box 1141
New Paltz
NY 12561

Websites
www.animalaid.org.uk
www.imperialcancer.co.uk
www.ivu.org
www.veggiepower.ca/

INDEX